The Early Days in Jackson Hole

The Early Days in Jackson Hole

by Virginia Huidekoper

GRAND TETON NATURAL HISTORY ASSOCIATION, MOOSE, WYOMING

The publication of this book was made possible in part by a grant from the Jackson Hole Preserve, Incorporated.

International Standard Book Numbers 0-931895-01-04 (Cloth Edition) and 0-931895-02-2 (Paper Edition)

Library of Congress Catalog Card Number 78-060201
Copyright 1978 by Virginia Huidekoper
All rights reserved. No portion of the contents of this book may be reproduced in any form without written permission of the publishers.
Published by the Grand Teton Natural History Association, Moose, Wyoming
in cooperation with the
Colorado Associated University Press
Boulder, Colorado
Print reproduction, Roger LaVake
Designed by Bruce Campbell
Duotones by George Waters
Composition by Elizabeth Typesetting Company
Printed by Viking Press, Inc., Minneapolis, Minnesota

Contents

Foreword and Acknowledgements

The history of Jackson Hole is much more than the usual tale of frontier life. The magnificent beauty of the Teton mountains and the richness of the surrounding country attracted people of diverse backgrounds and interests, and to an extent dominated their lives. Together the explorers, trappers, sportsmen, settlers and visitors created a colorful history, unique in character and influence.

The human history of Jackson Hole is the story of how a country of great natural beauty was used, treated, and in some areas, preserved. Fortunately many skilled photographers, both professional and amateur, made their way to this Teton country in the first few decades of settlement and left an accurate, as well as beautiful, documentation of the times.

Many of the photographs in this book were preserved in established archives. However, a good share came from family albums, shoe boxes, trunks and wallets, and were handed down through generations.

The greatest pleasure in collecting these photographs came from visits with old friends in the valley who went through their pictures and memories with me. There was a good deal of laughter and twinges of sadness when we viewed the past together. There was talk of hardship but more often tales of fun in "the old days." It was typical of the way they lived that these friends were eager to share their view of Jackson Hole with the rest of the world. To them we all owe gratitude.

For their contribution, support and encouragement I would particularly like to thank the following: W. C. Lawrence, Almer Nelson, Donald and Gladys Kent, Vilate Seaton Morris, Howard Schofield, John and Dorothy Yokel Waldron, Frances and Paul Judge, Pauline Goe Jillson, Hildegard Crandall, Richard Francis, Evelyn Cherry, Parthenia Stinnett, Helen and George Fleming, Marion Nethercott, William Balderston, Lee Vande Water and Houston Simpson, Thomas Lamb, the Holly Leek family, Dr. Donald G. MacLeod, Haynes Foundation, Mildred Capron, Eugene Hoffman, Dr. Elizabeth R. Brownell, Lee Lundy, White Grass Ranch and Triangle X Ranch.

Teton County Historical Society, Wyoming State Archives, University of Wyoming Western History Research Center, Grand Teton National Park and Teton National Forest.

Much credit for this publication belongs to Roger LaVake, whose interest in the book matches his skill in the darkroom; Zaidee Huidekoper, assistant printmaker and mindreader; Jody Byrd, organizer and typist; and Cammie Pyle, copy editor, proofreader and cook.

Preparing a permanent file of historical photographs was made possible through grants from the Jackson Hole Bicentennial Committee, Jackson State Bank and Teton County Museum Board.

Most of the pictures that appear in this book were included in the photographic exhibit "The Early Days in Jackson Hole," displayed at the Jackson Lake Lodge during the summer of 1976.

I am indebted to Vernon Johnson, executive manager, Grand Teton Lodge Company, 1976, for his support. To the trustees of Jackson Hole Preserve, Incorporated, who thought the subject worthy of publication, my thanks.

Virginia Huidekoper

When known, the photographers are credited for their work. The full names of these photographers, in order of appearance, are: William Henry Jackson, F. Jay Haynes, Benjamin Sheffield, Steven Nelson Leek, George and Bert Schofield, James Harper Teppan, Harrison Crandall, William Balderston, J.E. Stimson, and M.W. Trester.

The First Photographs

Over one hundred years ago, photographer William H. Jackson aimed his camera at the high peaks. Gently he removed the cap covering the lens. The Teton range, heretofore known only to a handful of frontiersmen and Indians, was mirrored on a wet, glass negative.

Photographing the Tetons in 1872 was not the easy matter it is today. A pioneer photographer had to be something of a chemist as well as a mechanic, artist and outdoorsman. Jackson was such a photographer.

Traveling with the Hayden Survey for the third time Jackson and a group of scientists broke off from the main part of the expedition to explore the mountains he had glimpsed from afar the previous year. Approaching from the West, the party camped in Teton Canyon. From there, Jackson and his assistant coaxed two pack mules over hazardous terrain to reach a high plateau facing the peaks.

He later wrote, "from the point gained by this precarious passage we had a glorious view. There was enough warmth in the sun's rays to melt snow so that we had a constant stream for washing photographic plates. I quickly set up my camera and began one of the busiest picture-making days of my whole career. It was one of those rare days when everything I wanted could be had with hardly a shift of the dark tent."

Six years later he traveled to Jackson's Hole (named after trapper Davey Jackson) and photographed the east side of the peaks. This was the first of Jackson's many visits to the valley.

JACKSON   The pioneer photographer's workshop on Table Mountain west of the Tetons.

JACKSON   "One of those rare days when everything I wanted could be had with hardly a shift of the dark tent," he wrote.

3

JACKSON   Hayden survey camp in Teton Canyon, 1872.

JACKSON   From the burnt slopes of Signal Mountain, the east side of the range was first photographed in 1878.

Early Sportsmen

The lure of fishing and big game hunting brought sportsmen to Jackson Hole long before the country was settled. In the late 1800s this land which the Indians and trappers had found so rich in wildlife became the location of elaborate hunting expeditions. Many wealthy outdoorsmen forfeited their usual African safaris for a new experience in the American West.

Guiding and outfitting these sportsmen became the most important occupation and greatest source of cash since the days of beaver trapping. Most early ranchers were involved in this pursuit part time, augmenting their meager incomes. However, guiding was much more than a means of earning money; most of those who chose this occupation thoroughly enjoyed the adventure and became expert observers of wildlife.

HAYNES   A visitor to Jackson Hole in 1883, President Chester A. Arthur spent several days in the valley enroute to Yellowstone. 175 pack animals were required to carry equipment and provisions. Above, Camp Hampton on the Snake River.

HAYNES   Railroad magnate W. Seward Webb hosted a spectacular hunting expedition that included four sportsmen, five guides, a U.S. General, twenty-four enlisted men and a camp crew. Pictured is the camp on the shore of Jackson Lake, 1897.

SHEFFIELD   Sighting in.

SHEFFIELD   The trophy.

SHEFFIELD   A spectacular catch, not unusual at the turn of the century.

12

SHEFFIELD   The rich reward of a hunting expedition, about 1910.

MOSER   Mrs. Moser and her maid, 1903.

SHEFFIELD   Dining in the wild country.

LEEK   Successful anglers.

16

The Elk

"The elk herd is the greatest single thing about the valley. Its history is that of the valley, and to a very real extent so is its fate ... "

Donald Hough

This elk (wapiti) herd ranging in Jackson Hole is the largest in North America. Numbering in the thousands, the elk have been sought after for food since prehistoric times. Sportsmen coveted the antlered heads for trophies and early settlers depended on the animals for survival.

Of all hazards, winter was the greatest threat to the herd. In 1909 severe weather caused the death of almost half the elk wintering near Jackson. Ranchers fed them what hay they could spare yet the loss was enormous.

Photographer Stephen N. Leek did much to arouse public interest in the plight of the elk. His photos and articles reached across the land.

In an effort to save the elk the state purchased $5,000 worth of hay. Later Congressional action and the Izaak Walton League provided the present National Elk Refuge which supports over 8,000 head on 24,000 acres.

LEEK

LEEK   Before the establishment of the National Elk Refuge, a large herd wintered in South Park.

19

LEEK   Ranchers fed all the hay that could be spared, but the desperate animals still raided fenced haystacks. The feed within reach was not enough to save them.

LEEK The state of Wyoming started a feeding program.

The Settlers

At the end of the nineteenth century Jackson Hole was dotted with the dwellings of settlers.

Lush grass and abundant water made the valley a natural for livestock production. This attracted a group of Mormon families who settled in South Park in 1889. More followed to homestead on Mormon Row (east of Blacktail Butte) and in the Wilson area. Up north trappers and guides located along the meandering streams and rivers to give ranching a serious try.

Others trickled in from all directions; Swiss, Germans, an Austrian and a couple of bachelors from Holland joined the Jackson Hole community. Some refugees from urban areas simply dropped into the Hole, accepted most any kind of occupation, and never left.

Industrious pioneers.

SCHOFIELD   Myrtle and the Foss brothers.

Returning from a cattle drive.

Ranching and Farming

More than any other activity, cattle ranching gave Jackson Hole its character. Hard work, independence and a sense of humor were the common denominators of the cattlemen and their ladies.

Because of the elements the job of raising a cow in this valley was never easy, but the grass was rich and produced prime quality beef for the market.

26

Lunch break. Sylvia Hansen and son Cliff.

Haying on the Si Ferrin Ranch, later known as the Elk Ranch.

Five mowers cut a wide swath.

29

SCHOFIELD   Rich land below Wilson.

LEEK   South Park potato growers.

Lee Lucas homestead, Spring Gulch.

Daily Living

"While I'm young this sort of life will be exciting and when
I get old I'll be used to it."

Bertha Chambers Gillette

TEPPAN Carrie Nesbitt on the Shive
Ranch east of Moran, about 1902.

SCHOFIELD Dave and
Bert, goose hunters.

SCHOFIELD Maude
Edmiston and little sister,
about 1913.

LEEK   The first Victrola in the valley, given to S. N. Leek by a magazine publisher in recognition of his efforts to save the elk.

LEEK   Dressed in Sunday best.

LEEK   Soulmates.

38

Twin moose calves, friends for the moment.

LEEK   Fourth of July celebration at South Park, 1890.

Celebrations

Life could be hard—ready money scarce—leisure was not taken lightly. Celebrations were a welcome break in the work routine.

The new Clubhouse was nearly completed when Jackson observed "the Fourth" in 1898.

LEEK   A fleet of celebrants on Jenny Lake.

A time for wearing "best clothes."

LEEK   Early rodeo in the open.

Rodeo

Rodeos are as much a part of Jackson Hole's heritage as the mountain men, trappers and hunters who came in over the passes.

In 1911 before the town of Jackson was even incorporated there was a forty-acre rodeo ground, complete with covered grandstand, right in the middle of town. It was here that the famous Jackson Hole's Frontier Days rodeo was held annually. It ranked right up there with the big shows at Cheyenne and Pendleton.

Throughout the summer, contests were held to "test stock" at Moran and the Elbo Ranch. These informal rodeos were primarily for the entertainment and edification of the dudes.

44

Action at the Elbo Ranch arena.

Grand entry. Jackson's Hole Frontier Days, 1913.

The all important structure was the judges' stand.

Exchanging horses in the relay race.

The first aeroplane to reach Jackson Hole landed at the rodeo grounds during Frontier Days.

Communities

Where people naturally met and gathered, communities evolved. The central features of most were the post office and school.

Travel between points in the valley was at best tedious and time consuming. Settlements enjoyed an independence from each other and a loyalty from their populace. Isolation was faced with characteristic good humor.

The Crail family operated the post office in 1910.

There have been eighteen official United States Post Offices in the history of Jackson Hole. Only six survive today.

A few became population centers—the remainder went away as quietly as the horse-drawn sleigh.

52

Mail and meals naturally went together since travelers often rode on the mail stage. Grovont Post Office, Mormon Row, 1910.

The post office was also a store and an agent for "American Ladies Tailoring Company."

Wilson

"Uncle Nick" Wilson, an adventurous sort, lived with the Indians as a youth, rode with the Pony Express, and led Mormon families over Teton Pass in 1889.

He built a cabin on the shore of Fish Creek, establishing the nucleus of the town of Wilson. His first wife, Matilda, opened the post office in 1898, and a son-in-law built a hotel and saloon. The town was ready to handle the increasing traffic of passengers and drivers making the trip "over the hill."

By tradition a spirited community, Wilson residents seemed to welcome any contest or task.

The hotel was built by Abraham Ward in 1898.

SCHOFIELD   Doing business in 1915.

Winter carnival parade.

The William Kelly homestead, 1910.

Kelly

William and Sophie Kelly homesteaded by the Gros Ventre River, raised cows, crops, cats, chickens and kids—and established a community. Sophie opened the Kelly post office in 1914. The town that grew around this center became a stopping place for ranchers driving to and from the summer range and headquarters for nearby settlers seeking supplies and conversation.

In the early summer of 1925 rancher Guil Huff was plowing a field near the Gros Ventre River, four miles above Kelly. The astonished man looked up to see the entire tree-covered mountainside above him moving toward the valley. He fled on a saddle horse, glancing back to see massive waves of earth surging across his fields. A few hours later Huff's house was floating on the lake created by the enormous landslide.

By 1927 Kelly boasted a population of 80 and was vying with Jackson for the county seat when fate intervened.

On the morning of May 18, 1927, the natural dam formed by the Gros Ventre landslide collapsed, releasing torrents of water from Slide Lake. The town was wiped out. Only the church and school remained. Six lives were lost and thousands of acres in the valley below were flooded. The Kelly family moved on to Idaho to start life anew.

58

Kent's Kelly Merc was the hub before the flood.

CRANDALL   A mountainside fell, June 23, 1925.

The day after the slide, Guil Huff stood atop his floating house.

Two years later the dam formed by the slide broke, flooding the Snake River Valley.

After the town was swept away, the Hilmar Bark house north of Kelly served as a temporary store and post office.

The Episcopal church, one of two buildings to survive the flood, was soon converted.

BALDERSTON   Dam construction, 1914. Sheffield's barn and cabins appear in the background.

Moran

Located at the outlet of Jackson Lake, the town of Moran had its beginning as headquarters for Ben Sheffield's fishing and hunting camp. Sheffield's Teton Lodge, cabins, barn and post office were there when the first Jackson Lake Dam, a wooden structure, was built in 1909.

The following year the dam washed away. Construction workers, building the concrete replacement and final enlargement in 1916, turned Moran into a bustling frontier town.

The Snake River Land Company acquired the townsite in 1928. It continued serving as a center for tourists and nearby ranchers until 1959 when it was dismantled and most of the buildings were moved to Colter Bay.

64

STIMSON   Rising water in the reservoir killed trees on the shoreline, creating one of the worst messes in the State's history.

In 1933 the cleanup began.

Horses were ferried across the lake to clear the shoreline.

CRANDALL   "I saw, each year, the increasing hordes of automobile tourists sweep the country like locusts." Struthers Burt, in the *Nation*, 1926.

Acquired by Rockefeller's Snake River Land Company in 1929, the Amoretti Inn became the original Jackson Lake Lodge.

TRESTER   The first known photograph of the town of Jackson, June 1, 1907. The Clubhouse is the prominent two-story structure.

Jackson

"Going to town" was a special occasion for the early settlers. They traded yarns as well as staples and knew some action was likely at any given time.

The Clubhouse (still standing on the east side of the square) was started before 1897 and served as a dance hall, social center and courtroom for the first trials—mostly game violations. Three other buildings, Anderson's hotel and post office, Foster's saloon and "Pap" Deloney's store stood when Jackson became a town in 1901.

A natural crossroad linking all ends of the valley, the Town of Jackson was destined to become famous for its entertaining frontier atmosphere.

70

LEEK Peter Nelson expanded the Hotel Jackson in 1905. The timber on Snow King Mountain (background) had been consumed by fire.

Top   The Jackson Mercantile began business in the Clubhouse building.

Bottom   Jackson State Bank, late 1920's. Robert Miller (second from left) was the founder.

Top Chester Simpson's hardware store was Jackson's first gas station, 1922.

Bottom LEEK   It was quite an occasion, July 8, 1926, when the Crown Prince and Princess of Sweden came to town. They were greeted by Yellowstone Park officials and William O. Owen (center). Later they dined at the Crabtree Hotel (left, background).

"Four Jacks and a Queen," 1912.

The Town Council, 1920-24. Jackson was the first town in the United States to be governed entirely by women. Mayor Grace Miller (center) had previously platted the town.

LEEK   St. John's Hospital.

Gambling was a big attraction during the dude era.

Contending with Nature

The mail leaves Wilson.

Winter

In the early days "wintering in" meant being self-sufficient and independent from the world. A few residents went "outside" for a spell, but real Jackson Holers saw it through, dealing cheerfully with the elements and finding adventure on most every outing.

Spring Gulch school bus.

Recess at Teton School, 1923.

SCHOFIELD Vesta Ward and Myrtle Schofield took to the slopes.

Dog races on the main street of Jackson.

Digging through a snowslide south of Jackson.

Bill Hackbarth landed on Jackson Lake.

Ice harvest on Jenny Lake.

SCHOFIELD   Both approaches to the "new" Snake River Bridge washed out in 1918.

The River

The great Snake River, running in many moods, ranged from benign to devastating. It nurtured the wily native trout, providing food for the Indians, trappers, and explorers, and game for the sportsmen. The high water of spring often threatened crops, livestock and people—it gnawed at bridges and barriers. At any season the river was unforgiving of human error.

Dividing the country of Jackson Hole physically, the river interrupted lines of communication and travel. Still it served as a waterway for the transport of goods and people. The Snake was both an aid and an obstacle, commanding awe and ingenuity.

88

High water flowed through Wilson.

SCHOFIELD   The river was the only means to transport lumber from Wilson to Hoback Junction.

Bill (W. D.) Menor started a farm, opened a store and built the Ferry at Moose shortly after his arrival in 1892.

A gurney wagon arrived at Scott's roadhouse on top of the pass.

Teton Pass

The "Pass" was the lifeline between Jackson Hole and the outside world in winter, and year around people and supplies came in via the railhead at Victor, Idaho.

Most important, everyone expected mail delivery service and despite snow slides, blizzards, high-centered horses and near frozen drivers, they got it. The freighters were a hearty breed—romantic figures undaunted by weather or unruly animals.

Wilson Price Hunt was the first reported white man to cross the well-beaten trail over Teton Pass in 1811. During the trapper era of the 1830s hundreds of men and thousands of animals went over the trail. In 1901 a wagon road was built at a cost of $500. The first automobile made the crossing on its own power in 1914.

92

Top   An upset on the way down.

Below   Making repairs in a blizzard, 1912.

New cars were transported over the pass on sleighs.

Gas coming over the pass.

SCHOFIELD the largest item hauled over the pass by 1912 was a flour mill destined for Kelly.

96

Automobiles made it "over the hill" in the late 1920's.

The Teton Mountains

Dominating the landscape for miles around, the Teton mountains were more than an awesome barrier between valleys. They became a landmark to natives and early explorers and were noted as "Pilot Knobs" on the maps of the Lewis and Clark expedition.

Imaginative trappers who wandered through the country in the 1830's sometimes referred to peaks as "tetons," a French slang expression meaning "breasts."

The Grand Teton became both a symbol and a challenge. In 1872 N. P. Langford and James Stevenson, members of the Hayden Survey accompanying W. H. Jackson on his photographic expedition, climbed the Grand Teton from the western side. This ascent was later disputed by W. O. Owen whose party found no evidence of a previous ascent when they reached the summit on August 11, 1898.

Although few local residents had the time or inclination to scale the peaks, by the late 1930s mountaineers from "outside" had reached the major summits.

Teton Glacier lured early mountaineers.

98

August 19, 1924, Geraldine Lucas, 59, was the first Jackson Hole woman to climb the Grand Teton. She carried the American flag on her back, unfurled it atop the peak, and weary though undaunted, posed for the camera.

Dudes

"A dude is one who comes in for weeks or months, stays at a dude ranch or something like it, dresses more like a cowhand than a cowhand does, and in a kind of simple minded way tries to fit into the country. The dude is in the minority (compared to the tourist)—he, and especially she, take up little space except when sitting down."

Donald Hough

SHEFFIELD   Dudes arriving at Sheffield's camp, about 1910. They traveled through Yellowstone from the railhead at Livingston, Montana.

Dudes departing from White Grass Ranch, heading for the train at Victor, Idaho.

First known lady dude wrangler, Katherine Yokel.

The original mixed drink.

MOSER   Bathing at Granite Creek, 1903.

CRANDALL   "Top railing" at Triangle X Ranch.

The Park

Ending a long controversy between local landowners and the government over its establishment, Grand Teton National Park was dedicated July 20, 1929.

In those first years a small but vigorous administration set about the task of making the new park accessible and accommodating. Although the depression was on, the park was able to build the fine trail system that exists today largely due to the aid of government CCC and WPA projects.

The original park boundary encompassed only the major peaks of the Tetons and the lake region at the foot of the mountains. The first expansion occurred (amidst general local protest) with the establishment of the Jackson Hole National Monument in 1943. The present boundary was created in 1950.

Both the original establishment and subsequent expansion of the park were in large measure due to the efforts of the late John D. Rockefeller, Jr. His interest and land donations played a significant part.

Top   Horace Albright, National Park Service Director, spoke at the dedication July 20, 1929.

Below   Park headquarters was established in a modest log building near Beaver Creek.

CRANDALL   The entire park staff in 1929, left to right, Naturalist Fritiof Fryxell, Superintendent and Mrs. Sam Woodring, Chief Ranger Edward Bruce and Ranger Phil Smith.

Road construction was a major project in the new park.

GRANT   A great trail was built along the skyline.

In 1931, John D., Jr., and Abby Rockefeller celebrated their 30th wedding anniversary boating on Jenny Lake.

CRANDALL Jenny Lake vista, early 1930's.

William Henry Jackson, age thirty, tintype.

116

About the Photographers

Since that day in 1872 when W. H. Jackson took his memorable photographs of the Tetons, many photographers, ranging from serious professionals to rank amateurs, have been drawn by the natural beauty of Jackson Hole and the character of the early residents. Among these photographers a few are notable for their significant contributions.

William Henry Jackson (1843-1942)

The great pioneer photographer William H. Jackson had a zest for adventure matched by prodigious energy. He interrupted a budding photographic career in Vermont with a youthful yen to wander. This led him to traverse the West as a bullwacker with a wagon train destined for California. On the return trip he lived the wild life of a vaquero, trailing mustangs from Los Angeles to the market in Omaha.

Following this adventure Jackson returned to his chosen vocation, photography. This time he chose Omaha as a place to begin life anew, because it was on the borderline between the East and the West, and was booming with activity connected with building the Union Pacific. In 1869 Jackson boarded the train as an itinerant photographer to follow the action of construction and picture views of interest along the way. The tracks had yet to reach Promontory.

Returning to Omaha, Jackson put his railroad scenes on display. A visitor to the studio, Dr. Ferdinand V. Hayden, leader of the United States Geological Survey, was impressed with Jackson's work and invited him to join the 1870 exploration of Wyoming and Utah territories. The following year the survey made an expedition to Yellowstone where Jackson took memorable photographs that revealed natural wonders of the area to a curious nation. These pictures had considerable influence on Congress which established Yellowstone as the first national park in the world.

Traveling with the survey again in 1872, Jackson and a few scientists made a side trip from the main route of the expedition to explore the west side of the Teton Range. Jackson later wrote, "the Tetons, never before photographed, now became of first importance as far as I was concerned." He photographed the peaks from a high plateau, making negatives 11x14, 8x10 and stereoscopic.

Jackson continued as photographer for the survey until it was disbanded in 1878. During this time he recorded the vast beauty of the remote Rockies and documented the rapidly disappearing scenes of Indian culture. His work of the survey period is notable for its scope, clarity of detail and masterful composition. To create these photographs, Jackson packed huge loads of cameras and equipment, often lugging them on his back when terrain became too hazardous for mules. The imposing San Juan mountains of Colorado inspired him to use a 20x24 camera, never before operated under rigorous outdoor conditions. "It is a wonder to me even now that I had the temerity to use it," he wrote fifty years later. All the negatives were developed on location using a dark tent or folding box for a darkroom.

Jackson later traveled to the Southwest and eventually ventured around the world. He returned to Jackson Hole in 1929 to photograph the dedication of Grand Teton National Park.

During a career that spanned the period from tintype to television Jackson amassed thousands of photographs. In his late years his interest turned to painting. Vigorous to the end, Jackson died at the age of ninety-nine.

F. Jay Haynes (1853-1921)

The stage was set for F. Jay Haynes when the Northern Pacific Railroad reached Puget Sound. Thousands of Americans were making a fast thrust into the northwestern frontier and Haynes branched out from his studio in Moorhead, Minnesota, to follow the action. He began his western trek photographing points of interest along the railroad and in 1880 became official photographer for the line.

With perception, Haynes used his camera to witness the transformation of prairies into farms, valleys into mining settlements and railroad stops into municipalities. He cleverly converted a passenger car into a studio to reach

F. Jay Haynes on the Missouri River, 1870.

Photographer Ben Sheffield with
Ben Jr. at his Moran headquarters.

boomtowns along the way. People flocked to his studio to have their portraits taken.

It was the remote country, however, that beckoned Haynes most. He was eager to take his chances with rivermen, mule drivers, Indians, guides and gold seekers scattered in the wilderness beyond reach of the trains. Everywhere he traveled, his cumbersome camera and equipment went with him. He took hundreds of photographs for his own satisfaction with no thought to their commercial value.

Venturing to Yellowstone in the 1880s, Haynes began the voluminous file of park photographs that would influence interest in the region all over the world. He became the official photographer of Yellowstone.

With his reputation as a master photographer and a skilled outdoorsman, Haynes was in demand to accompany exploring and sporting expeditions. His first documented trip to Jackson Hole was in 1883 when he was the only non-military member of the elaborate party accompanying President Chester A. Arthur on his trip through the valley enroute to Yellowstone. Haynes visited the Teton country again in 1896-97 when he joined railroad magnate W. Seward Webb who was hosting an extravagant sporting expedition in search of elk. Haynes' photographic assignments led him to explore the Canadian frontier and Alaska. He eventually operated three studios in Yellowstone, and added a stagecoach service to his concession.

During his career Haynes used each development in photography as it came, from collodion wet plates to color negatives. After fifty years as a photographer, he turned the studio over to his son, Jack, who followed him in the profession.

Benjamin D. Sheffield (1863-1946)

Ben Sheffield was only twelve years old when he left the security of the family hearth, hired on with a sheep outfit, and trailed a herd from Oregon to Montana Territory. Locating near Livingston, he made contacts with early sporting expeditions heading through the newly created Yellowstone National Park to seek big game in the rich country of Jackson Hole. He guided his first party into the valley in 1890.

Acquiring a ranch near old Moran, Sheffield went into the outfitting business in earnest. Wanting to offer more than just a hunting camp, he proceeded to build a set of snug cabins and then added the Teton Lodge, a hostelry that was to become famous for its bed and board. Sheffield's ranch and his ability at guiding attracted wealthy Americans and European noblemen.

Sheffield met his "dudes" at the railhead in Livingston. From there they would whirl through Yellowstone in white-topped buggies, shift to horseback at the south border, then board a motor launch (the valley's first) at Jackson Lake inlet for the final leg of the journey to Moran. On the whole it was an adventuresome trip. Sheffield recorded the activity with his 8x10 camera, managing to keep a good supply of glass negatives handy. On the hunting and fishing trips to follow he was seldom without his photographic equipment. One camera he had fitted with a gunstock so that he could quickly "aim and fire" without the need for a tripod.

Sheffield took hundreds of photographs but only a few of the glass negatives survive to this day. These, with their fine detail and varied subject matter, have become valuable in scientific research.

Stephen N. Leek (1858-1943)

Stephen N. Leek, Nebraska native, came to Jackson Hole in 1889, lured by reports of lush mountain country and abundant wildlife. He and a companion intended to trap for a living. The two men spent a bitter winter camped on the north shore of Jackson Lake where they cut aspen shoots for horsefeed and somehow survived. The reward for this hardship was a plentiful catch from their trapline. In the spring, Leek's share of the bear hides brought enough money to purchase a homestead in South Park.

Leek settled down to ranch and raise a family. However his interest in wildlife and skill in the outdoors led him to the big game outfitting business. He built a rustic lodge on the shore of Jackson Lake, a place that became a mecca for fishermen and a base for hunting operations.

One of the early sportsmen to frequent Leek's hunting camp was George Eastman, recent inventor of the Kodak camera (1888). Eastman was so impressed with Leek's guiding ability and uncommon interest in the welfare of wildlife that he presented him with a fine view camera, a gift that had a far reaching effect on Jackson Hole. From that time on Leek took photographs whenever and wherever he could. His subjects ranged from wildlife and flora to scenes of childhood. He managed to divert enough of his meager earnings to purchase additional photographic equipment,

CAPRON Stephen N. Leek in later years.

eventually acquiring stereo and panoramic cameras, and from France, a Pathé motion picture camera, the first in the valley.

Since a large part of the Jackson Hole elk herd wintered in the vicinity of his ranch, Leek seized the opportunity for spectacular pictures. Often he would camouflage himself in white to work his way in close to the animals. In hunting season he would follow animals more with his lens than with gunsight.

Skills that Leek acquired with his camera were put to dramatic use in the winter of 1909 when severe storms and scant feed decimated the elk herd. He used photographs and writing to describe the scenes of starvation. His accounts were published nationally; the prestigious New York Museum of Natural History featured an exhibit of Leek's telling photographs. Public attention was aroused, resulting in a feeding program and the eventual establishment of the National Elk Refuge.

Just as W. H. Jackson's photographs had influenced the National Park idea, Leek's pictures had a lasting effect on wildlife conservation.

123

Brothers Bert, left, and George Schofield.

Bert and George Schofield (1889-1939, 1891-1957)

Brothers Bert and George Schofield grew up on a homestead south of Wilson where they helped the family turn wild meadows into lush hayfields and produce cattle for the market. Schooling didn't take much of their time; they finished the eight grades available at Wilson.

It is unclear what motivated Bert and George to delve into photography. They ordered the camera outfit, which they shared, from a Sears Roebuck catalog in 1910. It included an Optima camera with a 6.3 lens and shutter up to 1/500th of a second, a set of glass negatives, chemicals and instructions.

Like many photographers of their day, the Schofields depended on night for a darkroom. Working at the ranch house, they used a kerosene lantern equipped with a red chimney for a safelight. Eventually they installed an enlarger.

The photos that the Schofields produced are notable for the subject matter and composition. Scenic photographs held little appeal to the brothers; instead they focused on family life and the vigorous activity associated with living in a mountain country. An adventurous family, the Schofields took time off for travel. Stowing all the necessities and the camera in a covered wagon, they spent a summer exploring Yellowstone. Another time they followed the wagon road west to Oregon.

In 1918 both Bert and George entered military service, and upon their return were engaged fulltime in the logging business. Their camera was carefully kept but seldom used again. The file of negatives that they amassed in eight years is not large, but the quality and scope are exceptional.

Harrison Crandall (1887-1970)

When he was a small boy attending grade school in Kansas, Harrison Crandall saw a photograph of the Teton mountains taken by William H. Jackson. The pull of this picture eventually led him to leave the family farm on the plains and move to Jackson Hole.

Early in life Crandall was determined to be a photographer, but earning a livelihood and military service during World War I interrupted the pursuit of his career. Nevertheless he was able to acquire formal art training along the way, first in Kansas and later at the Los Angeles School of Art. There he painted theater backdrops and murals to help pay for his education.

A chance to work for the U. S. Biological Service at Boise, Idaho, brought Crandall to the Rockies. He stayed at this job just long enough to buy a Model T Ford and head for the Tetons.

With his bride, Hildegard, Crandall arrived in Jackson Hole in spring, 1922. All their possessions, including a 3A Special Eastman camera and everything needed to live in the wilderness were piled high in the Model T. The summer was spent photographing, printing postcards by sunlight, developing them in a tent and washing them in the lakes. Sales of these postcards enabled them to survive. His professional career as a photographer had begun.

The Crandalls acquired a homestead near Jenny Lake and together they built an attractive log building for a studio. With his camera Harrison climbed to the high reaches of the peaks and hiked through the backcountry to record the beauty of places inaccessible to most. He photographed vistas, panoramic views and people. When Grand Teton National Park was established in 1929, Crandall, with his large file of pictures, was ready to meet the demand. Thousands of visitors took the Tetons home with them in the form of sparkling Crandall photographs.

Harrison Crandall in the high Tetons.

Notes

A typical list of equipment carried by an expeditionary photographer of the early 1870s actually included on one trip:

Stereoscopic camera with one or more pairs of lenses
5 x 8 Camera box plus lenses
11 x 11 Camera box plus lenses
Dark tent
2 Tripods
10 lbs. Collodion
36 oz. Silver nitrate
2 quarts Alcohol
10 lbs. Iron sulfate (developer)
Package of filters
1 1/2 lbs. Potassium cyanide (fixer)
3 yds. Canton flannel
1 Box Rottenstone (cleaner for glass plates)
3 Negative boxes
6 oz. Nitric acid
1 quart Varnish
Developing and fixing trays
Dozen and a half bottles of various sizes
Scales and weights
Glass for negatives, 400 pieces

This was the equipment of W. H. Jackson on his first trip with the Hayden Survey.

From "Photography and the American Scene," by Robert Taft.

Sources of Photographs

Page 2 University of Wyoming Archives (UWA), 3-5 Grand Teton National Park (GTNP), 8-9 Haynes Foundation, 10-13 GTNP, 14 Teton County Historical Society (TCHS), 16 UWA, 15 GTNP, 18-21 UWA, 24 TCHS, 25 Howard Schofield, 26 Evelyn Cherry, 27 Parthenia Stinnett, 28-29 Triangle X Ranch, 30 Howard Schofield, 31 UWA, 32 Simpson-VandeWater collection, 33 Frances Judge, 34-35 Howard Schofield, 36 Fern Wilson Hoffman, 37-38 UWA, 39 TCHS, 40 UWA, 41 TCHS, 42 UWA, 43 TCHS, 44 UWA, 45 TCHS, 46 Teton National Forest (TNF), 47 TCHS, 48 Vilate Seaton Morris, 49 TNF, 52 W.C. Lawrence, 53-54 Donald and Gladys Kent, 55 Richard Francis, 56 Howard Schofield, 57 Dorothy Yokel Waldron, 58 W.C. Lawrence, 59 White Grass Ranch, 60 above, Harrison Crandall family, below, W.C. Lawrence, 61 Parthenia Stinnett, 62 Donald and Gladys Kent, 63 Helen Fleming, 64 William Balderston, 65-69 GTNP, 70 Frances Judge, 71 UWA, 72 TCHS, 73 above, Simpson-VandeWater collection, below, UWA, 74 Donald and Gladys Kent, 75 TCHS, 76 UWA, 77 Pauline Goe Jillson, 80 Vilate Seaton Morris, 81 Parthenia Stinnett, 82 Vilate Seaton Morris, 83 Howard Schofield, 84 George Fleming, 85 Marion Nethercott, 86 W.C. Lawrence, 87 Virginia Huidekoper, 88 Howard Schofield, 89 Lee Lundy, 90 Howard Schofield, 91 GTNP, 92 Evelyn Cherry, 93 above, White Grass Ranch, below, TNF, 94-95 Evelyn Cherry, 96 Howard Schofield, 97 TNF, 98-99 GTNP, 102 GTNP, 103 White Grass Ranch, 104 Dorothy Yokel Waldron, 105 White Grass Ranch, 106 TCHS, 107 Harrison Crandall family, 110-115 GTNP, 116 UWA, 119 Haynes Foundation, 120 W.C. Lawrence, 123 Mildred Capron, 124 Howard Schofield, 127 Harrison Crandall family, Endpiece, Howard Schofield.

About the Author

Virginia Huidekoper has lived most of her life in Jackson Hole, Wyoming. A devotion to the Teton country and its people prompted her to compose this book. "These old photographs deserve to be shown for their beauty alone," she observes, "in addition, they recount history without the bias that writers are apt to have."

Author Huidekoper has had a varied career in Jackson Hole. She co-edited the county's weekly newspaper in the mid-forties and, twenty-five years later, founded the *Jackson Hole News*, a paper that emphasizes photographs of the country as well as news coverage.

An avid skier, hiker and horsewoman, these pursuits have taken her to the top of many major peaks (including the Grand Teton), and into most of the backcountry surrounding Jackson Hole. She operates a ranch near Wilson where her three children grew up, "with all the advantages of rural life and the stimulation of mountain country." Local politics and community affairs have always attracted her interest.

A professional airplane pilot for many years, Virginia claims this experience has given her a different perspective on history. "I can identify with W. H. Jackson when I look down on the ledges where he worked," she remarked.

Retired now from the newspaper business, Virginia just completed a "handmade, homegrown" log house where she expects to continue her work on historical subjects.